Handy Texas Genealogy Handbook

Gary L. Morris

ISBN-13: 978-1507786277

ISBN-10: 1507786271

Table of Contents

Notes

Genealogical Research in Texas

Because of its long and eventful history, there are many historical and genealogical records and resources available for tracing your family history in Texas. Because of the abundance of information held at many different locations, tracking down the records for your ancestor can be an ominous task. Don't worry though, we know just where they are, and we'll show you which records you'll need, while helping you to understand:

1. What they are
2. Where to find them
3. How to use them

These records can be found both online and off, so we'll introduce you to online websites, indexes and databases, as well as brick-and-mortar repositories and other institutions that will help with your research in Texas. So that you will have a more comprehensive understanding of these records, we have provided a brief history of the "Lone Star State" to illustrate what type of records may have been generated during specific time periods. That information will assist you in pinpointing times and locations on which to focus the search for your Texas ancestors and their records.

A Brief History of Texas

Spanish explorer Alonso Alvarez de Pineda was the first European to enter Texas when he sailed into the mouth of the Rio Grande in 1519. The Spanish considered Texas too far away from their colonies in the Mexico highlands and Florida however, and it wasn't until more than 160 years later that the first settlement was established at Ysleta del Sur in 1682. almost a decade before the earliest East Texas missions. But was 500 mi (800 km) from anything else resembling a settlement in Texas, and the Spanish considered it a part of New Mexico. Even then Ysleta was so remote that the Spanish considered it a part of New Mexico.

The establishment of Ft. St. Louis by La Salle on the Gulf coast in 1685 changed the attitude of the Spanish towards the colonization of Texas, and in 1689 Capt. Alonso de León authorized an expedition to expel the French. A Coahuilan priest, Father Damien Massanet, accompanied the León expedition and was ordered to establish a mission near wherever a fort was built. Over the next several decades the two men and those who succeeded them established a string of mission-forts across Texas. In 1718, the Spanish commenced building a fort, San Antonio de Bexar, and a mission, San Antonio de Valero, at the site of the present city of San Antonio.

The US had shown no interest in Texas until the Louisiana Purchase in 1803. With Louisiana a neighbor to Texas, the era of the "filibusters" (military adventurers) arose. The filibusters began to filter across the border into Spanish territory, and although they were mostly trading horses with the Native Americans, the Spanish saw them as a threat to Spanish sovereignty. These filibusters, along with pirates and various Anglo-Americans would play an important part in the Mexican Revolution for the independence of Texas from 1810-1821.

After the Spanish deserted Texas in 1821, it became a province of Mexico. San Antonio and Goliad were the only towns of significance, and the population was made up mostly of Native Americans. In 1820, Moses Austin of Missouri had been given permission by Spanish authorities to introduce Anglo-American settlers into Texas, presumably as a protection against aggression by the United States. The new Mexican government upheld the agreement, and soon three hundred families were settled in the area between the Brazos and Colorado Rivers. Others soon followed, and between 1821 and 1835 the non-Indian population had risen from 7,000 to between 40,000 and 50,000.

Religious and social unrest between the Anglo-American immigrants and the Mexicans led to the Mexican Congress enacting the Law of 1830, which forbade the majority of immigration and imposed duties on all imports. The Texan Anglos reacted with much the same anger as the New Englanders had once done when England imposed severe and unfair taxes on the original American colonies. The Anglo-Texans insisted they were not opposing the Mexican nation, but rather Mexican political excesses. They put their hope in Gen. Antonio López de Santa Anna, who was leading a liberal revolution against then Mexican President Anastasio Bustamante.

In 1833 Santa Anna became president of Mexico and almost immediately dropped his liberal position. The Texans sent Stephen F. Austin, who had succeeded his late father as head of the colonization movement to Mexico City to petition Santa Anna to strike the Law of 1830, to allow English to be used to conduct public business, and to make Texas a separate state. Austin was arrested on his way back to Texas and imprisoned for a year. Santa Anna attempted to enforce customs collections but his officials were resisted by colonists led by William Barret Travis, drove the Mexican officials out of the town of Anahuae. Santa Anna responded by placing Texas under military jurisdiction, and when Mexican soldiers attempted to take a cannon from colonists in the town of Gonzales on October 2, 1835, the Texas Revolution began.

The Texans formed a provisional government and sent three commissioners to Washington D.C to request aid form the United States. The Mexican army crossed the Rio Grande in 1836 and focused on a mission-fort known as the Alamo. There, 187 Texans under the command of Colonel William Barret Travis, prepared to resist the Mexican onslaught. The defenders held off the Mexican forces until March 6 and only succumbed after 4,000 troops stormed the fort, ending with the death of every defender, including twp American legends – Davy Crockett and James Bowie.

Texas issued a declaration of independence four days after the battle, and when 342 Texans who had surrendered to Santa Anna's forces at Goliad on the 27 March 1836, were slaughtered instead of treated as prisoners of war, the Texan fight for independence intensified. At San Jacinto (modern day Houston), 800 Texans under the command of Sam Houston surprised the Mexican army numbering 1,600 during their siesta period. The Mexicans lost 630 soldiers with a further 280 wounded, and the remainder taken prisoner. Texan losses were 9 killed and 30 wounded. It was at this decisive victory, which freed Texas from Mexico forever, that the famous battle cry "Remember the Alamo" was born.

For 10 years Texas struggled as an independent republic, its debt increasing ten-fold during that period, and it wasn't until joining the Union on 19 February 1846 that any hope of prosperity existed. That hope lasted only until the coming of the Civil War, at which time Texas followed its southern neighbors into the Confederacy. Little fighting took place on Texas soil during the war, though the last battle at Palmito Ranch near Brownsville took place on Texas ground on May 13, 1865. Amazingly that was more than one month after General Lee's surrender at Appomattox House in Virginia. A military force governed Texas briefly during Reconstruction, and then by a Republican regime. It was during this period that the so-called carpetbag constitution was passed in 1869 giving the franchise to blacks, which in turn gave rise to a group determined to deny them that right, the Ku Klux Klan.

Texas was readmitted to the union on March 30, 1870, and a new constitution was approved in 1976. Developments in the cattle industry saw the Texas economy flourish, and the discovery of the Spindletop oil field—the state's first gusher—in 1901, and the subsequent development of the petroleum and petrochemical industries, brought immense riches to the area.

Important Dates in Texas History

1641 – Spanish Governor appointed for Texas

1682 – First settlement established at Ysleta del Sur near modern day El Paso

1700 – Mission of San Juan Bautista founded

1749 – Laredo founded

1813 – Spain crushes rebellion for independence at San Antonio

1821 – Ceded from Spain to Mexico

1836 – Battle of the Alamo, Texas becomes a Republic

1845 – Statehood

1861 – Secedes from Union (February 1)

1870 – Readmitted to Union (March 30)

Famous Battles Fought in Texas

Ultimately the most famous battle fought on Texas soil was the **Battle of the Alamo**, fought between Mexican troops and Texans in 1836. Other important battles during the Texan War for Independence were the **Battle of Refugio**, March 14 1836, and the **Battle of San Jacinto**, April 21, 1836.

The battle accounts that exist can be very effective in uncovering the military records of your ancestor. They can tell you what regiments fought in which battles, and often include the names and ranks of many officers and enlisted men.

Battle of the Alamo: http://www.historynet.com/battle-of-the-alamo

Battle of Refugio:
http://www.tamu.edu/faculty/ccbn/dewitt/goliadsanpat2.htm

Battle of San Jacinto: http://www.history.com/this-day-in-history/the-battle-of-san-jacinto

Common Texas Genealogical Issues and Resources to Overcome Them

Boundary Changes: Boundary changes are a common obstacle when researching Texas ancestors. You could be searching for an ancestor's record in one county when in fact it is stored in a different one due to historical county boundary changes.

The **Atlas of Historical County Boundaries** can help you to overcome that problem. It provides a chronological listing of every boundary change that has occurred in the history of Texas.

Atlas of Historical County Boundaries:
http://publications.newberry.org/ahcbp/documents/TX_Consolidated_Chronology.htm#Consolidated_Chronology

Name Changes: Surname changes, variations, and misspellings can complicate genealogical research. It is important to check all spelling variations. Soundex, a program that indexes names by sound, is a useful first step, but you can't rely on it completely as some name variations result in different Soundex codes. The surnames could be different, but the first name may be different too. You can also find records filed under initials, middle names, and nicknames as well, so you will need to **get creative with surname variations** and spellings in order to cover all the possibilities. For help with surname variations read our instructional article on **How to Use Soundex**.

get creative with surname variations:
http://obituarieshelp.org/blog/?p=634

How to Use Soundex: http://obituarieshelp.org/blog/?p=505

Texas Genealogical Organizations and Archives

Genealogical resources include not only records, but the organizations that house them, or can direct you to them. These institutions include: *Archives, Libraries, Genealogical Societies, Family History Centers, Universities, Churches, and Museums.*

Following are links to their websites, their physical addresses, and a summary of the records you can find there.

Archives and Libraries

Texas State Library and Archives - Vital statistics indexes s to Texas births, deaths, marriages and divorces, Index to Confederate Pension Applications, Texas Adjutant General Service Records, 1836-1935, Republic Claims - claims for payment, reimbursement, or restitution submitted by citizens to the Republic of Texas government from 1835 through 1846, Confederate Indigent Families Lists, Texas County Tax Rolls, Index of County Records (Naturalizations, Deeds, Wills, Probates, County Census, County Vital records), City Directories,
Newspapers, 1867 Voters' Registration, Texas Convict Record Ledgers and Indexes, Republic of Texas Passports.

1201 Brazos St.
Austin TX 78701
Tel :(512) 463-5455
Email: info@tsl.texas.gov

Mailing Address:
P.O. Box 12927
Austin TX 78711-2927

Texas State Library and Archives:
https://www.tsl.texas.gov/arc/genfirst.html

National Archives Southwest Region (Ft. Worth) - Federal population censuses for all States, 1790-1930 (including indexes for 1880, 1900, 1910, and 1920); military service records, pension and bounty land warrant applications; passenger arrival records; Dawes census cards and enrolment jackets for the Five Tribes of Oklahoma

2600 West 7th Street
Suite 162
Fort Worth, TX, 76107
Telephone: 817-831-5620
Fax: 817-334-5621

National Archives Southwest Region (Ft. Worth):
http://www.archives.gov/fort-worth/public/

Clayton Library Center for Genealogical Research - County and state histories, abstracts of wills, deeds, marriages, court minutes, vital records, church, cemetery records and colonial collections of several states, city directories for major US cities through 1910, City of Houston Death Records, Census Records, Ship passenger lists, naturalization records, periodicals, and family histories

5300 Caroline
Houston, TX 77004
Telephone: 713-284-1999

Clayton Library Center for Genealogical Research:
http://www2.houstonlibrary.org/clayton/index.html

Houston Public Library – Historical newspapers, Cemetery records, Civil War resources, African American research resources, Houston city directories, Trans-Atlantic Slave trade database

500 McKinney Street
Houston, Texas 77002
Tel: 832-393-1313

Houston Public Library: http://houstonlibrary.org/genealogy

Fort Worth Library – Federal census, books, periodicals, Texas County Tax Lists, historical photograph collection, school and college yearbooks, obituary index, and various online databases

500 W. Third St.
Fort Worth, TX 76102-7305
Tel: 817-392-READ (7323)
Email: genlhst@fortworthtexas.gov (Genealogy Questions)

Fort Worth Library:
http://fortworthtexas.gov/library/info/default.aspx?id=24852

Ralph W. Steen Library (Stephen F. Austin State University) – Excellent genealogy collection featuring lots of material on the pre-Civil War era, and many county court records which include wills and probates

1112 North St.,
Nacogdoches TX 75962
Phone: (936) 559-2970

Ralph W. Steen Library: http://library.sfasu.edu/

Genealogical and Historical Societies

Genealogical and historical societies have access to extensive catalogues of genealogical data. They are also able to offer expert guidance for genealogical researchers. Many members are professional genealogists who are most willing to share their expertise in finding ancestors.

Texas State Genealogical Society – Family histories, research assistance, and genealogy resources

c/o Scott Fitzgerald, Treasurer
PO Box 7308
Tyler, TX 75711-7308
Phone: (903) 539-5572
Fax: (903) 592-6782

Texas State Genealogical Society:
http://www.rootsweb.ancestry.com/~txsgs/

The San Antonio Genealogical & Historical Society – Bexar County Cemetery records, Marriage Books, obituaries collection, county census records, historical photograph collection, research library containing over 17,000 books

PO Box 790087
San Antonio TX 78279-0087
Tel: 210-342-5242
Email: saghs@sbcglobal.net

The San Antonio Genealogical & Historical Society:
http://www.rootsweb.ancestry.com/~txsaghs2/

North Texas Genealogical Association - Marriage Announcements, Obituaries, Funeral Home records

PO Box 4602
Wichita Falls, TX 76308
E-mail: info@ntgatrailtracers.org

North Texas Genealogical Association:
http://www.ntgatrailtracers.org/

Texas State Historical Association – Digital library with lots of resources for researching the Texas Revolution era

Texas State Historical Association: http://www.tshaonline.org/

Texas Mailing Lists

Mailing lists are internet based facilities that use email to distribute a single message to all who subscribe to it. When information on a particular surname, new records, or any other important genealogy information related to the mailing list topic becomes available, the subscribers are alerted to it. Joining a mailing list is an excellent way to stay up to date on Texas genealogy research topics. Rootsweb have an extensive listing of **Texas Mailing Lists** on a variety of topics.

Texas Mailing Lists:
http://lists.rootsweb.ancestry.com/index/usa/TX/misc.html

Texas Message Boards

A message board is another internet based facility where people can post questions about a specific genealogy topic and have it answered by other genealogists. If you have questions about a surname, record type, or research topic, you can post your question and other researchers and genealogists will help you with the answer. Be sure to check back regularly, as the answers are not emailed to you. The Texas message boards at **Rootsweb** are completely free to use.

Rootsweb:
http://boards.rootsweb.com/localities.northam.usa.states/mb.ashx

Texas Newspapers and Periodicals

Many genealogy periodicals and historical newspapers contain reprinted copies of family genealogies, transcripts of family Bible records, information about local records and archives, census indexes, church records, queries, land records, obituaries, court records, cemetery records, and wills. The following sites have historical Texas newspapers and periodicals that you can search online or on-site.

Texas State Library and Archives – Hundred's of historical newspapers on microfilm dating from 19th century to modern era

1201 Brazos St.
Austin TX 78701
Tel:(512) 463-5455
Email: info@tsl.texas.gov

Mailing Address:
P.O. Box 12927
Austin TX 78711-2927

Texas State Library and Archives:
https://www.tsl.texas.gov/arc/genfirst.html

Clayton Library Center for Genealogical Research - over 3000 genealogy and local history periodical titles

5300 Caroline
Houston, TX 77004
elephone: 713-284-1999

Clayton Library Center for Genealogical Research:
http://www2.houstonlibrary.org/clayton/index.html

University of Texas Arlington Central Library - Good newspapers collection from Texas and across the United States including the Texas Digital Newspaper program which features newspapers from over seventy Texas counties, ranging in date from 1829 to 2012.

702 Planetarium Place
Arlington, TX 76019
Telephone: 888-565-9023
E-mail: library-ref@uta.edu

University of Texas Arlington Central Library:
https://www.uta.edu/library/index.php

Fort Worth Library – The Fort Worth Gazette November 1, 1883 to January 1, 1888

500 W. Third St.
Fort Worth, TX 76102-7305
Tel: 817-392-READ (7323)
Email: genlhst@fortworthtexas.gov (Genealogy Questions)

Fort Worth Library:
http://fortworthtexas.gov/library/info/default.aspx?id=24852

GenealogyBank.com – free searchable database of Texas newspaper archives, 1813-1993

GenealogyBank.com:
http://www.genealogybank.com/gbnk/newspapers/explore/USA/Texas/

The Online Books Page – links to historical Texas books and periodicals available for viewing online

The Online Books Page: http://onlinebooks.library.upenn.edu

Library of Congress Digital Newspaper Directory – free searchable database of historical U.S. newspapers dating from 1690-present

Library of Congress Digital Newspaper Directory: http://chroniclingamerica.loc.gov/search/titles/

NewspaperArchive.com – largest online database of historical newspapers in the world.

NewspaperArchive.com: http://newspaperarchive.com/

Historical Texas Maps and Gazetteers

Maps are an integral part of genealogical research. They help us to locate landmarks, towns, cities, parishes, states, provinces, waterways and roads and streets. They also help us to determine when and where boundary changes might have taken place, and give us a visualization of the area we're researching in.

For locating place names, a gazetteer is the best possible resource for any genealogist. Gazetteers are also sometimes called "place name dictionaries", and can help you to locate the area in which you need to conduct research. Below are links to the maps and gazetteers for research in Texas.

Peabody GNIS Service – Texas:
http://peabody.research.yale.edu/cgi-bin/Query.GNIS?ST=Texas&SU=1

Color Landform Atlas – Texas:
http://fermi.jhuapl.edu/states/tx_0.html

1985 U.S. Atlas: http://www.livgenmi.com/1895/TX/

Texas Hometown Locator: http://texas.hometownlocator.com/

Texas City Directories

City directories are similar to telephone directories in that they list the residents of a particular area. The difference though is what is important to genealogists, and that is they pre-date telephone directories. You can find an ancestor's information such as their street address, place of employment, occupation, or the name of their spouse. A one-stop-shop for finding city directories in Texas is the **Texas Online Historical Directories** which contains a listing of every available online historical directory related to Texas. Another useful site is **US City Directories** which identifies printed, microfilmed, and online Texas directories and their repositories.

Texas Online Historical Directories:
https://sites.google.com/site/onlinedirectorysite/Home/usa/tx

US City Directories: http://www.uscitydirectories.com/sd.htm

Some archives and libraries that have both digitized and microfilmed city directories for Texas are:

Texas State Library and Archives – Vast collection of City Directories dating from 1875 to modern era

1201 Brazos St.
Austin TX 78701
Tel:(512) 463-5455
Email: info@tsl.texas.gov

Mailing Address:
P.O. Box 12927
Austin TX 78711-2927

Texas State Library and Archives:
https://www.tsl.texas.gov/arc/genfirst.html

Houston Public Library – Houston City directories dating from 1866

500 McKinney Street
Houston, Texas 77002
Tel: 832-393-1313

Houston Public Library: http://houstonlibrary.org/genealogy

Texas Genealogical Records

Birth, Death, Marriage and Divorce Records – Also known as vital records, birth, death, and marriage certificates are the most basic, yet most important records attached to your ancestor. The reason for their importance is that they not only place your ancestor in a specific place at a definite time, but potentially connect the individual to other relatives. Below is a list of repositories and websites where you can find Texas vital records.

Early Texas Birth, Death, and Marriage records may be found in Texas **County Courts**, while Divorce records can be found in Texas county **District Courts**.

County Courts: https://admin.county.org/about-texas-counties/county-websites/Pages/default.aspx

District Courts: https://admin.county.org/about-texas-counties/county-websites/Pages/default.aspx

Texas Department of State Health Services - Births or deaths that have occurred in Texas from 1903 to the present,

Vital Statistics Unit
1100 West 49th Street
Austin, TX 78756

Vital Statistics Unit:
http://www.dshs.state.tx.us/vs/reqproc/birth_death_general.shtm

Texas State Library and Archives - Birth indexes from 1903 through the most recent year available, delayed birth indexes that include births as early as 1880, cumulative index for the years 1903 through 1909, and index beginning with 1910 with each year is indexed separately

1201 Brazos St.
Austin TX 78701
Tel:(512) 463-5455
Email: info@tsl.texas.gov

Mailing Address:
P.O. Box 12927
Austin TX 78711-2927

Texas State Library and Archives:
https://www.tsl.texas.gov/arc/vitalfaq.html

Ralph W. Steen Library (Stephen F. Austin State University) – County Birth, death, marriage, and divorce records dating from mid-19th century

1112 North St.,
Nacogdoches TX 75962
Phone: (936) 559-2970

Ralph W. Steen Library: http://library.sfasu.edu/

The San Antonio Genealogical & Historical Society – Bexar County Marriage Books dating from mid-19th century

PO Box 790087
San Antonio TX 78279-0087
Tel: 210-342-5242
Email: saghs@sbcglobal.net

The San Antonio Genealogical & Historical Society:
http://www.rootsweb.ancestry.com/~txsaghs2/

Family Search has the following indexes that can be searched online for free:

Texas, Birth Certificates, 1903-1935:
https://familysearch.org/search/collection/1803956

Texas, Birth Index, 1903-1997:
https://familysearch.org/search/collection/1949342

Texas, Births and Christenings, 1840-1981:
https://familysearch.org/search/collection/1681015

Texas, County Marriage Index, 1837-1977:
https://familysearch.org/search/collection/1803987

Texas, County Marriage Records, 1837-1977:
https://familysearch.org/search/collection/1803985

Texas, Death Index, 1903-2000:
https://familysearch.org/search/collection/1949337

Texas, Death Index, 1964-1998:
https://familysearch.org/search/collection/1375599

Texas, Deaths and Burials, 1903-1973:
https://familysearch.org/search/collection/1681049

Texas, Deaths, 1890-1976:
https://familysearch.org/search/collection/1983324

Texas, Deaths, 1977-1986:
https://familysearch.org/search/collection/1930157

Texas, Divorce Index, 1968-2010:
https://familysearch.org/search/collection/2038378

Texas, Marriages, 1837-1973:
https://familysearch.org/search/collection/1681052

Texas, Marriages, 1966-2010:
https://familysearch.org/search/collection/2031191

Census Records

Census records are among the most important genealogical documents for placing your ancestor in a particular place at a specific time. Like BDM records, they can also lead you to other ancestors, particularly those who were living under the authority of the head of household.

Texas State Library and Archives – County census records dating from 1830

1201 Brazos St.
Austin TX 78701
Tel:(512) 463-5455
Email: info@tsl.texas.gov

Mailing Address:
P.O. Box 12927
Austin TX 78711-2927

Texas State Library and Archives:
https://www.tsl.texas.gov/arc/genfirst.html

Fort Worth Library – Federal census 1850-1930

500 W. Third St.
Fort Worth, TX 76102-7305
Tel: 817-392-READ (7323)
Email: genlhst@fortworthtexas.gov (Genealogy Questions)

Fort Worth Library:
http://fortworthtexas.gov/library/info/default.aspx?id=24852

National Archives Southwest Region (Ft. Worth) - Federal population censuses for all States, 1790-1930 (including indexes for 1880, 1900, 1910, and 1920)

2600 West 7th Street
Suite 162
Fort Worth, TX, 76107
Telephone: 817-831-5620
Fax: 817-334-5621

National Archives Southwest Region (Ft. Worth):
http://www.archives.gov/fort-worth/public/

Clayton Library Center for Genealogical Research - Census Records from 1830
5300 Caroline
Houston, TX 77004
elephone: 713-284-1999

Clayton Library Center for Genealogical Research:
http://www2.houstonlibrary.org/clayton/index.html

The **Free Census Project** has transcribed many Texas indexes and new material is added daily

Free Census Project: http://usgwcensus.org/cenfiles/tx.htm

Access Genealogy – Texas county census records dating from 1860

Access Genealogy: http://www.accessgenealogy.com/census/texas-census-records.htm

African American Census Schedules Online – slave schedules, mortality schedules, slave-owners census

African American Census Schedules Online:
http://www.afrigeneas.com/aacensus/ga/

Native Americans in Census Records (US National Archives)

Native Americans in Census Records:
http://www.archives.gov/research/census/native-americans/

Texas Church Records

Church and synagogue records are a valuable resource, especially for baptisms, marriages, and burials that took place before 1900. You will need to at least have an idea of your ancestor's religious denomination, and in most cases you will have to visit a brick and mortar establishment to view them.

Most church records are kept by the individual church, although in some denominations, records are placed in a regional archive or maintained at the diocesan level. Local Historical Societies are sometimes the repository for the state's older church records. Below are links archives that maintain church records, as well as a few databases that can be viewed online.

The **Family History Library** contains many church records from a variety of denominations on microfilm.

Family History Library:
http://familysearch.org/learn/wiki/en/Family_History_Library

Central Repositories for Denominational Records

Church of Jesus Christ of Latter-day Saints (Mormons)

Early Mormon Church records for Texas can be found on film located at the LDS Family History Library in Salt Lake City and can be searched via the **Family History Library Catalog**

Family History Library Catalog:
https://familysearch.org/eng/Library/FHLC/frameset_fhlc.asp

<u>Baptist</u>

Southwestern Baptist Theological Seminary
A. Webb Roberts Library
2001 West Seminary Drive
Fort Worth, TX 76122
Phone: (817) 923-1921 (x3330)
Fax: (817) 921-8754

Southwestern Baptist Theological Seminary:
http://www.swbts.edu/academics/libraries/

Baylor University
Moody Memorial Library
Box 6307
Waco, TX 76703
Phone: (254) 710-2111
Fax: (254) 710-3116

Moody Memorial Library: http://www.baylor.edu/lib/centrallib/

<u>Lutheran</u>

James R. Crumley, Jr. Archives
Lutheran Theological Southern Seminary
4201 North Main Street
Columbia, SC 29203
Telephone: 803-786-5150 x234
E-mail: archives@ltss.edu

James R. Crumley, Jr. Archives: http://crumleyarchives.org/

Disciples of Christ

Brite Divinity School Collection
Mary Couts Burnett Library
Texas Christian University
2913 West Lowden
Fort Worth, TX 76129
Phone: (817) 921-7117
Fax: (817) 921-7447

Mary Couts Burnett Library: http://www.library.tcu.edu/

Presbyterian

Presbyterian Historical Society
425 Lombard Street
Philadelphia, PA 19147
Telephone: 1-215-627-1852
Fax: 1-215-627-0509

Presbyterian Historical Society: http://www.history.pcusa.org/

Methodist

Center for Methodist Studies
United Methodist Historical Collection
Bridwell Library
Southern Methodist University
6005 Bishop Boulevard
P.O. Box 750476
Dallas, TX 75275

Center for Methodist Studies:
http://www.smu.edu/bridwell/Collections/SpecialCollectionsandArc
hives/CenterforMethodistStudies

Roman Catholic

Diocese of Amarillo
P.O. Box 5644
Amarillo, TX 79117
Phone: (806) 383-2243

Diocese of Amarillo:
http://www.amarillodiocese.org/index.cfm?load=page&page=152

Diocese of Austin
6225 Highway 290 East
Austin, TX 78723-1025
Phone: (512) 949-2400

Diocese of Austin: http://www.austindiocese.org/

Diocese of Beaumont
P.O. Box 3948
Beaumont, TX 77704-3948
Phone: (409) 924-4300

Diocese of Beaumont: http://dioceseofbmt.org/

Diocese of Brownsville
1910 University Blvd.
Brownsville, TX 78520
Phone: (956) 550-1517

Diocese of Brownsville: http://www.cdob.org/

Diocese of Corpus Christi
620 Lipan
Corpus Christi, TX 78401
Phone: (361) 693-6726

Diocese of Corpus Christi: http://www.diocesecc.org/

Diocese of Dallas
3725 Blackburn St.
Dallas, TX 75219
Phone: (214) 528-2240

Diocese of Dallas:
https://www.cathdal.org/pages/History_and_Archives

Diocese of El Paso
499 St. Matthews St.
El Paso, TX 79907
Phone: (915) 872-8400

Diocese of El Paso: http://elpasodiocese.org/diocese/

Diocese of Ft. Worth
800 West Loop 820 South
Fort Worth, TX 76108
Phone: (817) 560-330

Diocese of Ft. Worth: http://www.fwdioc.org/

Archdiocese of Galveston-Houston Archives
P.O. Box 907
Houston, TX 77001
Phone: (713) 652-8283

Archdiocese of Galveston-Houston Archives:
http://www.archgh.org/archives/

Diocese of Larado
1901 Corpus Christi Street
Laredo, TX 78043
Phone: (956) 727-2140

Diocese of Larado: http://www.dioceseoflaredo.org/

Diocese of Lubbock
4620 Fourth Street
Lubbock, TX 79499-8700
Phone: (806) 792-3943

Diocese of Lubbock: http://catholiclubbock.org/beta.htm

Diocese of San Angelo
804 Ford Street
San Angelo, TX 76905
Phone: (325) 651-7500
Mailing Address: P.O. Box 1829
San Angelo, TX 76902-1829

Diocese of San Angelo:
http://www.sanangelodiocese.org/index.html

Archdiocese of San Antonio
2718 W. Woodlawn
San Antonio, TX 78228
Phone: (210) 734-2620

Archdiocese of San Antonio: http://www.archsa.org/

Diocese of Tyler
1015 ESE Loop 323
Tyler, TX 75701-9663
Phone: (903) 534-1077

Diocese of Tyler: http://www.dioceseoftyler.org/index.php

Diocese of Victoria
P.O. Box 4070
1505 E. Mesquite Lane
Victoria, TX 77901
Phone: (361) 573-0828

Diocese of Victoria: http://www.victoriadiocese.org/

Catholic Archives of Texas
1600 North Congress
Capitol Station P.O. Box 13327
Austin, TX 78711-3327
Phone: (512) 476-4888
Fax: (512) 469-9537

Catholic Archives of Texas: http://www.catholicarchivesoftx.org/

Texas Military Records

More than 40 million Americans have participated in some kind of war service since America was colonized. The chance of finding your ancestor amongst those records is exceptionally high. Military records can even reveal individuals who never actually served, such as those who registered for the two World Wars but were never called to duty.

Below are a number of links to websites and archives that contain Texas military records.

Texas State Library and Archives - Index to Confederate Pension Applications, Texas Adjutant General Service Records, 1836-1935, Confederate Indigent Families Lists.

1201 Brazos St.
Austin TX 78701
Tel:(512) 463-5455
Email: info@tsl.texas.gov

Mailing Address:
P.O. Box 12927
Austin TX 78711-2927

Texas State Library and Archives:
https://www.tsl.texas.gov/arc/genfirst.html

National Archives Southwest Region (Ft. Worth) - Military service records, pension and bounty land warrant applications

2600 West 7th Street
Suite 162
Fort Worth, TX, 76107
Telephone: 817-831-5620
Fax: 817-334-5621

National Archives Southwest Region (Ft. Worth):
http://www.archives.gov/fort-worth/public/

US Department of Veterans Affairs Nationwide Gravesite Locator – includes information on veterans and their family members buried in veterans and military cemeteries having a government grave marker.

US Department of Veterans Affairs Nationwide Gravesite Locator: http://gravelocator.cem.va.gov/

Family Search has the following indexes which are searchable online for free:

Texas, Civil War Service Records of Confederate Soldiers, 1861-1865: https://familysearch.org/search/collection/1932381

Texas, Civil War Service Records of Union Soldiers, 1861-1865: https://familysearch.org/search/collection/1932425

You may also find your ancestor's military records in the following databases:

United States General Index to Pension Files, 1861-1934: https://familysearch.org/search/collection/1919699

United States Index to Service Records, War with Spain, 1898: https://familysearch.org/search/collection/1919583

United States Index to Indian Wars Pension Files, 1892-1926 – military pension records of soldiers who fought in the Indian Wars between 1817 and 1898

United States Index to Indian Wars Pension Files, 1892-1926: https://familysearch.org/search/collection/1979427

United States Registers of Enlistments in the U.S. Army, 1798-1914 - index of men who enlisted in the United States Army, 1798-1914.

United States Registers of Enlistments in the U.S. Army, 1798-1914: https://familysearch.org/search/collection/1880762

United States Mexican War Pension Index, 1887-1926 - index to Mexican War pension files for service between 1846 and 1848

United States Mexican War Pension Index, 1887-1926: https://familysearch.org/search/collection/1979390

Civil War Soldiers Service Records - Service records for both Union and Confederate soldiers indexed by soldier's name, rank, and unit.

Civil War Soldier Service Records: http://go.fold3.com/civilwar_records/

Texas Cemetery Records

As convenient as it is to search cemetery records online, keep in mind that there are a few disadvantages over visiting a cemetery in person. They are:

- Tombstone information is not always accurately transcribed
- The arrangement of the graves in a cemetery can be crucial as family members are often buried next to each other or in the same grave. This arrangement is not always preserved in the alphabetical indexes that are found online.

With that information in mind, the following websites have databases that can be searched online for Texas Cemetery records.

Clayton Library Center for Genealogical Research – Large cemetery transcription and burial records database for the entire state of Texas

5300 Caroline
Houston, TX 77004
Telephone: 713-284-1999

Clayton Library Center for Genealogical Research:
http://www2.houstonlibrary.org/clayton/index.html

Family Search has the following indexes which can be searched online for free:

Texas, Bexar County, San Antonio Cemetery Records, 1893-2007: https://familysearch.org/search/collection/1828544

Texas, Houston, Historic Hollywood Cemetery Records, 1895-2008: https://familysearch.org/search/collection/2040173

See Also:

Texas Tombstone Transcription Project - death and burial records

Texas Tombstone Transcription Project:
http://www.usgwtombstones.org/texas/texas.html

African American Cemeteries Online – African American, slave, and Native American cemetery records

African American Cemeteries Online:
http://africanamericancemeteries.com/

Access Genealogy – database of Texas cemetery record transcriptions

Access Genealogy:
http://www.accessgenealogy.com/cemetery/texas-cemetery-records.htm

Find a Grave – over 100 million grave records can be searched on this site. Search can be conducted by name, location, or cemetery name.

Find a Grave: http://www.findagrave.com/

Interment.net - A free online database containing approximately 4 million cemetery records from around the world.

Interment.net: http://www.interment.net/

Billion Graves – as the name implies, you can search a billion records including headstone photos, transcriptions, cemetery records, and grave locations.

Billion Graves:
http://billiongraves.com/pages/search/index.php#cemetery

Texas Obituaries

Obituaries can reveal a wealth about our ancestor and other relatives. You can search our **Texas Obituaries Listings** from hundreds of Texas newspapers online for free.

Texas Obituaries Listings:
http://obituarieshelp.org/texas_newspaper_obituaries.html

Texas Wills and Probate Records

The documents found in a probate packet may include a complete
inventory of a person's estate, newspaper entries, witness testimony,
a copy of a will, list of debtors and creditors, names of executors or
trustees, names of heirs. They can not only tell you about the
ancestor you're currently researching, but lead to other ancestors.

Texas State Library and Archives – County Wills, Deeds, and
Probate records, including Court Minutes dating from 1830's to mid-
twentieth century.

1201 Brazos St.
Austin TX 78701
Tel:(512) 463-5455
Email: info@tsl.texas.gov

Mailing Address:
P.O. Box 12927
Austin TX 78711-2927

Texas State Library and Archives:
https://www.tsl.texas.gov/arc/genfirst.html

Clayton Library Center for Genealogical Research - Abstracts of
wills and deeds

5300 Caroline
Houston, TX 77004
elephone: 713-284-1999

Clayton Library Center for Genealogical Research:
http://www2.houstonlibrary.org/clayton/index.html

Ralph W. Steen Library (Stephen F. Austin State University) – County probate records, deeds, and wills dating from mid-19th century

1112 North St.,
Nacogdoches TX 75962
Phone: (936) 559-2970

Ralph W. Steen Library: http://library.sfasu.edu/

Family Search has the following indexes that can be searched online for free:

Texas, Coleman County Records, 1849-2008:
https://familysearch.org/search/collection/1930271

Texas, Comanche County Records, 1858-1955:
https://familysearch.org/search/collection/1831470

Texas, Concho County Records, 1849-2008:
https://familysearch.org/search/collection/1930272

Texas, Eastland County Records, 1868-1949:
https://familysearch.org/search/collection/1911179

Texas, Mills County Clerk Records, 1841-1985:
https://familysearch.org/search/collection/1837923

Texas, Nolan County, Civil Court Minutes and Case Files, 1881-1938: https://familysearch.org/search/collection/1425534

Texas, Probate Records, 1800-1990:
https://familysearch.org/search/collection/2016287

Texas, Swisher County Records, 1879-2012:
https://familysearch.org/search/collection/2103490

Texas Immigration and Naturalization Records

The naturalization process generated many types of records, including petitions, declarations of intention, and oaths of allegiance. These records can provide family historians with information such as a person's birth date and place of birth, immigration year, marital status, spouse information, occupation, witnesses' names and addresses, and more.

If your ancestor lived in or near a large city, or near a city where U.S. courts convened, you may find naturalization records in the **U.S. District Court** before 1906.

U.S. District Court:
http://www.uscourts.gov/FederalCourts/UnderstandingtheFederalCo
urts/DistrictCourts.aspx

For the rural areas of Texas, naturalization records may be found with the **County Clerk** in each county. Often the records were mixed in with other court proceedings making them difficult to locate. A few counties kept separate records for naturalization. After 1906, all naturalizations were handled in Federal District Courts.

County Clerks: https://admin.county.org/about-texas-counties/county-websites/Pages/default.aspx

Clayton Library Center for Genealogical Research - Ship passenger lists, Texas naturalizations

5300 Caroline
Houston, TX 77004
elephone: 713-284-1999

Clayton Library Center for Genealogical Research:
http://www2.houstonlibrary.org/clayton/index.html

Texas State Library and Archives – Naturalizations, Declarations of Intent dating from 1830's to post World War II era.

1201 Brazos St.
Austin TX 78701
Tel:(512) 463-5455
Email: info@tsl.texas.gov

Mailing Address:
P.O. Box 12927
Austin TX 78711-2927

Texas State Library and Archives:
https://www.tsl.texas.gov/arc/genfirst.html

National Archives Southwest Region (Ft. Worth) - Passenger arrival records

2600 West 7th Street
Suite 162
Fort Worth, TX, 76107
Telephone: 817-831-5620
Fax: 817-334-5621

National Archives Southwest Region (Ft. Worth):
http://www.archives.gov/fort-worth/public/

US National Archives – Immigration records, Naturalization records, Ship's Passenger lists

The National Archives and Records Administration
8601 Adelphi Road
College Park, MD 20740-6001
Tel: 1-866-272-6272; 1-86-NARA-NARAS

US National Archives: http://www.archives.gov/research/guide-fed-records/groups/085.html

Family Search has the following indexes which can be searched online for free:

Texas, Eagle Pass Arrival Manifests and Indexes, 1905-1954: https://familysearch.org/search/collection/1916041

Texas, El Paso Manifests of Arrivals at the Port of El Paso, 1905-1927: https://familysearch.org/search/collection/2120714

Texas, Laredo Arrival Manifests, 1903-1955: https://familysearch.org/search/collection/2038112

Texas, Naturalization Records, 1906-1989: https://familysearch.org/search/collection/1389983

Texas Native American Records

National Archives Southwest Region (Ft. Worth) - Dawes census cards and enrollment jackets for the Five Tribes of Oklahoma

National Archives Southwest Region (Ft. Worth):
http://www.archives.gov/fort-worth/public/

Access Genealogy – Texas Native American census records, tribal histories, and much more

Access Genealogy: http://www.accessgenealogy.com/native/texas-indian-tribes.htm

U.S. National Archives - information on American Indians who maintained their ties to Federally-recognized Tribes (1830-1970).

U.S. National Archives: http://www.archives.gov/research/native-americans/

Records of the Bureau of Indian Affairs (BIA):
http://www.archives.gov/research/guide-fed-records/groups/075.html

American Indians Records Repository - records dating from the 1700s including trust, education and other historic Indian Affairs records

American Indian Records Repository
Meritex Enterprises
17501 West 98th Street
Lenexa, KS 66219
Phone: 913-888-0601

American Indians Records Repository:
http://www.doi.gov/ost/records_mgmt/american-indian-records-repository.cfm

Missing Matriarchs – Resources for Researching Female Texas Ancestors

Looking for female ancestors requires an adjustment of how we view traditional records sources. A woman's identity was often under that of her husband, and often individual records for them can be difficult to locate. The following resources are effective in locating female ancestors in Texas where traditional records may not reveal them.

Bibliographies

1. *Women in Early Texas,* Evelyn M. Carrington (Jenkins Publishing Co., 1975)
2. *We Just Toughed it Out: Women Heads of Household on the Llano Estacado, 1880-1935, Georgellen Burnett (Texas Western Press, 1989)*
3. *Claiming Their Own Land: Women Homesteaders in Texas,* Florence C. Gould (Texas Western Press, 1991)
4. *Read All About Her! Texas Women's History: A Working Bibliography, Elizabeth Snapp (Texas Women's University Press, 1996)*

Selected Resources for Texas Women's History

Daughters of the Republic of Texas Library
PO Box 1401
San Antonio, TX 78295-1401

Foundation for Women's Resources
3500 Jefferson, Suite 210
Austin, TX 78731

Women's Collection
Blagg-Huey Library
Texas Women's University
TWU Station
Box 23925
Denton, TX 76204

Common Texas Surnames

The following surnames are among the most common in Texas and are also being currently researched by other genealogists. If you find your surname here, there is a chance that some research has already been performed on your ancestor.

Adams, Allison, Allman, Anthony, Armstrong, Arney, Arny, Arrowood, Arthurs, Asbill, Ashford, Austin, Bailey, Baldwin, Barfield, Barlow, Baugus, Beaslely, Bennett, Bertram, Bigbee, Binkley, Bird, Blackwell, Blanchard, Bloom, Boggess, Boggus, Boyer, Bradley, Bradshaw, Bragg, Brandon, Breanon, Brice, Bridges, Bridgett, Brondon, Brooking, Brooks, Brown, Brtram, Buchanan, Buchannon, Bumpass, Bunch, Burk, Burton, Cain, Callahan, Calloway, Campbell, Carr, Carroll, Cartlidge, Cartwright, Cates, Caudle, Cayle, Chapman, Chappell, Clark, Clements, Coble, Cockrell, Collier, Cook, Cooper, Copeland, Cornelius, Cowden, Cox, Dalton, Daniels, Davis, Dawson, Dixon, Dodson, Donnelson, Doyle, Dunbar, Duncan, Dunkin, Dyer, Easley, Easterling, Eberhart, Elden, Ellen, Elliott, Elmore, Erskine, Estell, Fickling, Finney, Foster, Francis, Freeman, Garcia, Gibson, Graham, Graves, Green, Griffith, Grimsby, Guinn, Haines, Hamilton, Hampton, Handy, Hankinson, Harris, Harvick, Hayman, Haymon, Head, Henderson, Higgins, Hill, Hindman, Holt, Hopkins, Hoskins, Huffman, Hull, Hunkapillar, Hunsucker, Hunt, Hunter, Ingram, Jackson, Jacquess, Jenson, Johns, Johnson, Jones, Jowers, Keathley, Keener, Keesee, Keithley, Kelley, Kelton, Kent, Key, King, Kiser, Knox, Lance, Lane, Langford, Langley, Lassetter, Layos, Layton, Lee, Leslie, Lewis, Limmer, Lindsay, Littrell, Lloyd, Looney, Lowery, Lyles, Mann, Mason, Matis, McCarty, McCommas, McCormack, McCurdy, McDaniel, McDaniels, McDonald, Mcfarland, McGarrah, McGee, McKeller, McRae, Miller, Mitchell, Moffitt, Moiser, Monetti, Moore, Moser, Mosier, Moss, Nail, Nalle, Newland, Norris, Norse, Norseworthy, O'Ryain, Osborn, Pardue, Parish, Parrish, Patterson, Payton, Pearson, Pearsons, Peters, Pharaoh, Phelts, Pierce, Plunk, Pointer, Pomeroy, Powles, Price, Race, Ramsey, Rangham, Rasmusson, Ray, Reel, Reese, Reinhardt, Renfro, Rhea, Rhod, Richardson, Richie, Riddick, Roberts, Robertson, Rogers, Rose,

Sabra, Sarceda, Scarbrough, Schmid, Seip, Sheets, Shuford, Sims, Sipes, Sizemore, Smith, Snider, Spann, Specht, Spicer, Spies, Spooner, Spouse, Spradlin, Steel, Stimpson, Stone, Stracener, Sullivan, Summitt, Sursa, Susan, Sutton, Symons, Tangren, Taylor, Tennyson, Thomas, Trae, Trammble, Trammell, Treadway, Trimble, Trimmer, Turner, Unknown, Vail, Vance, Viles, Wale, Walker, Wallace, Walton, Watson, Watts, Weaver, Weekley, Welch, Wells, White, Whitefield, Whitehead, Wilcoxson, Williams, Williant, Wilson, Windsor, Winebrinner, Withem, Woody, Wright, Young, Zimmerman

About the Author

Gary L. Morris worked from 2009 to 2014 as a professional researcher for a major player in the genealogy field. After tracing his family lineage back to 1683, he found that genealogy could be an expensive undertaking. As such, has decided to publish these helpful guides to share the valuable free information he has discovered during his career to help others trace their family lineages as inexpensively as possible. An avid genealogist himself, he hopes you will find this guide factual, thorough, helpful, and most of all, effective in helping you to find your family members.

Notes

Notes

www.ingramcontent.com/pod-product-compliance
Lightning Source LLC
Chambersburg PA
CBHW071130280526
45787CB00003B/1225